501 /

GW01071799

This book

Poverty and
Free Trade in Mexico

Belinda Coote

OXFAM
LIBRARY

✓ 500

NAFTA Poverty

and Free Trade

in Mexico

Belinda Coote

Oxfam Publications

© Oxfam (UK and Ireland) 1995

A catalogue record for this book is available from the British Library

ISBN 0 85598 302 7

Published by Oxfam (UK and Ireland)
274 Banbury Road, Oxford OX2 7DZ, UK
(registered as a charity, no. 202918)

Available in Ireland from Oxfam in Ireland, 19 Clanwilliam Terrace, Dublin 2; tel. 01 661 8544.

Available in Canada and the USA from Westview Press, 5500 Central Avenue, Boulder, Colorado 80301, USA; tel. (303) 444 3541; fax (303) 449 3356.

Co-published in Australia by Community Aid Abroad, and available from them at 156 George Street, Fitzroy, Victoria 3065, Australia; tel. +61 3 289 9444; fax +61 3 419 5318/5895.

Designed and typeset by Oxfam Design Department OX1550/PK/94
Printed by Oxfam Print Unit
on environment-friendly paper
Set in 10/12.5 point Palatino with Franklin Gothic Book and Demi

Contents

NAFTA: Poverty and Free Trade in Mexico

Introduction

In January 1994 the North American Free Trade Agreement (NAFTA) came into effect, linking Mexico, the United States, and Canada in a pact to increase trade and investment. The agreement is of special significance, because it is the first of its kind to link countries from the 'developed' and 'developing' worlds.

For Mexico the NAFTA represents another step down the road of economic liberalisation which its government has been pursuing for more than a decade. For the United States, it is the first stage in its wider policy objective of creating a hemispheric free-trade zone stretching from the Port of Anchorage in the far north to Tierra del Fuego in the extreme south. There is no shortage of candidates for membership, with governments from all over the region queuing up to join. The NAFTA thus has implications for countries far beyond its three initial signatories.

The purpose of this report is to look at the impact of the Mexican government's economic liberalisation policies, and the NAFTA, on the people of Mexico. It is hoped that the lessons learned from their experiences will inform those in other countries where similar policies are being pursued, and help to achieve policy changes in favour of the poor.

The Chiapas uprising

On 1 January 1994 guerrilla forces in Mexico's southern state of Chiapas declared war on the Mexican government. The guerrilla army, consisting of indigenous peasants, announced themselves as the Zapatista National Liberation Army, after Emiliano Zapata, the Indian leader of the 1910 Mexican revolution. On declaring war, they delivered a statement to news media, threatening to march on Mexico City unless the government met their demands for equal treatment for peasants. The statement declared:

For [the government] it does not matter that we possess nothing, absolutely nothing, not a home, not land, not work, not education. We will not halt our combat until the needs of our people are satisfied. The dictators have been leading a war of genocide against native peoples for years.[1]

Few people in Mexico were surprised by this development, for Chiapas is one of Mexico's poorest and most troubled states, despite its rich oil reserves. The 3.2 million people who live there (approximately 4 per cent of Mexico's total population[2]) are mainly indigenous Indians of Mayan descent. But Chiapas is also home to many thousands of Guatemalan refugees. To escape from war, poverty, and maltreatment in their own country, they have been living in camps along the state's border with Guatemala since the late 1970s.

The basic services provided in Chiapas are insufficient to meet the needs of its own population, let alone those of the refugees, and infrastructural development is minimal. The state has one of the highest rates of illiteracy in Mexico, reflecting both the inadequate provision of schools in the region and the government's failure to provide an education system appropriate to the needs of a multi-ethnic and multi-lingual society. Health-care facilities are limited, there are few roads, and communications are poor.

Mexico's sweeping land-reform programmes of the 1930s had little impact on Chiapas. The best land in the region has remained concentrated in the hands of a few wealthy landowners, mostly engaged in large-scale coffee production and raising cattle for export. Most of the population scratch a living from tiny plots of marginal land, growing basic food and cash crops such as coffee, maize, and beans. Disputes over land between the landlords and peasants have been numerous and often violent. The *status quo* is maintained by the region's corrupt political and judicial systems, which are fashioned to protect the interests of the landowners. As a result, the peasants have no recourse to social or economic justice through democratic means. Poverty in the region has been intensified by the collapse in international commodity prices in the 1980s, which hit peasant producers of coffee and basic food staples hard. Such conditions made fertile breeding ground for the discontent which led to the uprising in January 1994.

The Zapatista National Liberation Army timed their declaration of war on the Mexican government to coincide with the official launching of the North American Free Trade Agreement, the NAFTA. It was a symbolic gesture to protest against the latest step down the road of an economic development strategy from which the vast majority of Mexico's population, but in particular its indigenous communities, are excluded. The Zapatista rebels, with their eloquently articulated demands for justice, democracy, and measures to alleviate acute poverty as preconditions for peace, have frustrated the government's efforts to project an image of Mexico as a peaceful, democratic country which recently joined the 'First World' club of the Organisation for Economic Co-operation and Development (OECD).

Opening up the Mexican economy

The NAFTA, which came into effect on 1 January 1994, is an agreement between the governments of Mexico, the United States, and Canada to phase out restrictions on the movement of goods, services, and capital between the three countries over a period of ten to fifteen years. For Mexico it locks into place the free-market reforms that its government has been pursuing since 1982 — policies which won it praise from the US International Trade Commission in 1990 for having made the transition from 'one of the world's most protected economies into one of the most open systems in just a few years'.[3]

The protectionist years

Until 1982, successive Mexican governments pursued policies of state-led industrialisation through import substitution. Manufacturing industry was built up with the help of state subsidies and protective tariffs. Similar policies were used to promote self-sufficiency in food through government support to small-scale producers, and through agrarian reform. Money saved on imports was pumped back into the economy to create new industries, and thus a new class of waged workers able to foster an expansion of the domestic market. In only a few decades Mexico had evolved from a mainly rural, agricultural nation to an industrialising and increasingly urban society. Between 1940 and 1970 it enjoyed annual economic growth of more than six per cent, which earned it praise as a model for state-led industrialisation in the developing world.[4]

These are often referred to as the 'miracle years' of Mexico's economic development, even though, by the mid-1960s, cracks were beginning to appear in its economic armoury. Decades of dependence on government support had made Mexican industry inefficient and uncompetitive, and increasingly reliant on imports. At the same time there was a decline in the country's

4

ability to feed itself. While, in the past, government support had successfully promoted small-scale production of basic grains, even more government resources had been pumped into the export-oriented capitalist sector, which benefited from state-financed irrigation projects and technical assistance. Vegetable and fruit exports to the USA boomed, and the extension of the country's livestock industry displaced crops for home consumption. As *per capita* food production fell, agricultural imports began to rise, contributing to a widening budget deficit. These developments coincided with a dwindling in Mexico's oil reserves. No longer sufficient to meet requirements, these had to be supplemented by imports — just as international oil prices were booming.

An oil-fuelled spending spree ...

By 1976 Mexico faced an economic crisis of huge proportions. The government embarked on an austerity programme in connection with a loan from the IMF. But in 1977 the country struck it rich with the discovery of new oil reserves. Renewed confidence in Mexico's economic future meant that foreign banks, flush with petro-dollars (recycled oil profits, mainly from the Middle East), lined up to lend it virtually unlimited amounts. The government went on a spending spree. The budget deficit widened and inflation soared. The private sector lost confidence in the economy, and the result was a massive flight of capital to more stable economies elsewhere. The government soon found that it was unable to cover its budget and could not meet the annual payments on its external debt, which was now one of the largest in the developing world.

... paid for by borrowing

By 1982 Mexico was on the brink of economic collapse. Oil prices were sinking and high interest rates on its foreign debt (now standing at $86 billion — up from $6 billion in 1970) meant that it faced huge debt-servicing requirements. At the same time its foreign-exchange reserves had been drained through private capital flight. The government had no choice but to appeal for help to the World Bank, the IMF, and the USA. The aid that flowed in throughout the 1980s was not without a price. The international financial community, led by Washington, demanded that Mexico restructure its economy along free-market lines. This would require a complete reversal of its former protectionist policies, to open up its economy to the forces of international competition. Waiting in the wings to direct this restructuring was a new generation of Mexican politicians and bureaucrats. They were from the ruling Institutional Revolutionary Party (PRI), but educated in the USA, and proponents of market liberalisation.

Deeper and deeper into debt

For the first few years, under the administration of PRI president Miguel de la Madrid, Mexico was a model debtor. It managed to impose the recommended financial adjustments and austerity measures, while keeping its debt repayments on track. But the debt crisis did not go away, and by 1985 the government was, once again, asking for emergency loans. To secure a new credit deal with Washington in 1986, Mexico agreed to a major restructuring of its economic policies, designed to accelerate the liberalisation of trade. The resulting reductions in tariffs and other restrictions on trade, and the liberalisation of foreign investment, were intended to create a business climate that would attract foreign investors, reverse capital flight, and open up new export opportunities. The government also brought Mexico into the General Agreement on Tariffs and Trade (GATT) in time for it to participate in the new Uruguay Round of trade negotiations launched that year. It saw the adoption of GATT trading guidelines as an important step towards building a new and vigorous export-oriented economy.

By 1988 the economy had begun to stabilise. Non-petroleum exports began to rise, mainly as a result of increased assembly-line production in the factories situated along the Mexico/US border. The results were trade surpluses and *per capita* growth for the first time since 1981. Newly elected President Salinas de Gortari pursued the neo-liberal reforms vigorously, throwing the country open to foreign trade and investment. However, none of this could disguise the essentially weak state of the Mexican economy; nor could it deal with the huge backlog of underemployed or unemployed workers left without decent jobs by the economic crisis of the 1980s. While exports continued to rise, imports were rising twice as fast, and very soon Mexico once again started to experience a negative trade balance. Nor did the country's massive debt burden go away. By late 1991 the country owed at least $16 billion more than it had done in 1982, when the crisis exploded.

The fear of isolation

As the decade drew to a close, the Salinas administration began to consider the advantages of integration with its closest and most important trading partner, the USA — which accounts for nearly 70 per cent of Mexican trade. There was also increased regionalism to consider. As Europe moved towards an integrated market and as Canada and the USA moved closer to signing a free-trade accord, Mexico became worried that it might be left out in the cold. Entering a regional trading bloc with its northern neighbour would ensure that the US market would stay open to Mexico-based exporters at a time of rising protectionist sentiment in the USA, and make Mexico an even more attractive investment prospect to US companies.

In August 1990 President Salinas formally applied to enter a free-trade deal with the United States. Six months later it was announced that Canada would join the negotiations for a tri-lateral trade accord. Formal negotiations for a North American Free Trade Agreement began in June 1991 and an agreement was announced on 12 August 1993. The agreement was granted legislative approval by the three governments concerned, in time for it to come into effect on 1 January 1994.

The North American Free Trade Agreement

The NAFTA created the largest free-trade zone in the world. It brings together 363 million people (compared with 326 million in the European Union) with a combined GDP of US$6.8 trillion. Its objectives are to eliminate trade barriers between the three countries, promote conditions of fair competition, increase investment opportunities, establish effective procedures for the resolution of disputes, and promote further trilateral, regional, and multilateral co-operation. To achieve this, it provides for the gradual elimination of tariff and non-tariff barriers against the movement of goods, services, and capital in the region over a period of 10 to 15 years.

To ensure that the benefits of the NAFTA are accorded only to goods produced in North America, strict rules of origin are specified in the agreement. These mean that goods may qualify for duty-free import or export within the region only if a high proportion of their production costs is added in North America. Intellectual property (such as copyrights and patents) is also dealt with in the agreement, which provides for strict protection of the patents of US companies.

The NAFTA provides for the creation of a Trade Commission to deal with the resolution of disputes. If the Commission fails to reach an agreement, a bilateral arbitration panel can be set up to ensure a speedy resolution.

Although the NAFTA clearly encompasses more than just trade, it is limited to issues strictly defined as business. Unlike the European Union agreement, the NAFTA does not create a common market for the movement of people. NAFTA's immigration provisions are limited to the 'reciprocal entry of business persons' under tightly defined categories.[5] The

8

agreement does, however, have two side-accords, on labour and the environment, which have been tacked on in an effort to enforce minimum standards. The USA and Mexico have also agreed to establish a North American Development Bank, to finance the clean-up of the border region, which has been badly polluted as a result of the Border Industrialisation Programme. In addition, the US government has set aside funds to retrain US workers who will lose their jobs as a result of the agreement.

In signing the agreement, the Mexican government hoped that integration with the US market will spur economic growth, generate employment, and allow its economy to take off in the same way as that of the 'four tigers' of Asia (Hong Kong, Singapore, Taiwan, and South Korea). The country's superior natural resources, its cheap labour, and its proximity to the United States, together with the advantages of a trilateral free-trade agreement, supposedly set the stage for this hoped-for transformation.

Opposition to the NAFTA

Once it became known that negotiations were under way to establish a free-trade agreement between Mexico, the United States, and Canada, there was wide-scale publicity on the subject in all three countries. Broad-based coalitions were formed in each, to challenge the NAFTA proposals. Some advocated outright rejection of the proposed agreement. Others argued for reform of various aspects of its provisions.

In the USA, opposition to the NAFTA came broadly from two opposing perspectives. One represented a narrow, nationalist view in favour of increased protectionism, mainly in the interests of preserving US jobs. The other took a broader development perspective, arguing that the high social and environmental costs that would occur on both sides of the Mexican border as a result of the agreement demonstrated the NAFTA to be a flawed development model. The ensuing debate was bitter and protracted, and split the Democratic Party, forcing Bill Clinton, in his election campaign, to promise side-accords on labour and the environment in an effort to reunite his party and counteract some of the negative aspects of the agreement.

In Mexico, a broad-based coalition was founded in early 1991, called the Mexican Action Network on Free Trade (RMALC). This coalition of independent unions, environmental groups, representatives from the small-business sector, and popular organisations expressed its concern that the NAFTA would subvert national sovereignty. It warned that the agreement would 'give a legal and permanent status to the subordination of national needs to the interests of large corporations and to the neo-liberal policies which have already cost our people so much'.[6]

Lessons from Canada

Most vociferous of those campaigning for an outright rejection of the deal were those coalitions which formed around the issue in Canada. They pointed to their country's experience of free trade with the United States. This had been provided for by the Free Trade Agreement (FTA), which came into effect in January 1989 and which paved the way, and provided the model, for the NAFTA.

The FTA was sold to the Canadian public on the grounds that it would promote economic development. However, the agreement has become highly controversial. Unable to compete with lower-cost US industry, many of the smaller Canadian manufacturing companies have closed down. Others have moved south across the border to take advantage of lower interest rates and lower social-benefit charges. There has been a record number of mergers, takeovers, closures, and 'rationalisations' of industry; thousands of jobs have been destroyed in the process. Unemployment is now officially 10 per cent, although unofficially estimated at 15 per cent.[7] By allowing US companies investment opportunities in Canada and by removing controls on exports, free trade with the USA is also threatening Canada's control over its own natural-resource base and its ability to conserve its environment. Canadians opposing the NAFTA argue that their own experiences prove that free trade carries high social and environmental costs, entails a loss of national sovereignty, while handing over considerable power to the corporate sector, and is of questionable economic benefit.

Prospects for the poor in Mexico

Opposition to the NAFTA in the USA and Mexico has tended to focus on specific aspects of the agreement, particularly those concerning the expected social and environmental costs. Yet at the heart of public concern lie the huge social, economic, and political disparities that exist between Mexico and its northern neighbours.

11

All the indicators show the increasing poverty and desperation of the Mexican people since the country embarked on its programme of economic reform in the early 1980s. According to official figures, half the Mexican population live in poverty, and one fifth in conditions of extreme poverty.[8] Since 1979 the buying power of real wages has fallen by nearly 60 per cent. Public expenditure on health care and education has fallen to half its 1980 level. Two thirds of the population are malnourished: Mexico's record in this respect is one of the worst in Latin America.[9]

In 1990 the World Bank estimated that one sixth of Latin America's poverty-stricken population lived in Mexico. It singled out four states where the problem was most serious, among them Chiapas, location of the 1994 uprising. Seventy per cent of the combined population of these states live below the poverty line. Half are illiterate, four times more than in regions with better economic conditions. Between 30 and 40 per cent lack access to health services, and 80 per cent are without safe drinking water.[10] These disparities are not peculiar to the states mentioned by the World Bank. In general, Mexico's rural population suffers disproportionately from high rates of unemployment and infant mortality, and lack of government resources. Such figures are a clear indication that the free-market economic policies pursued by the government since 1982 have failed the poor.

Increasingly, poverty in Mexico has served to accentuate many of the disparities that exist between Mexico and its northern neighbours in areas such as health care, education, and basic living standards. In addition there are huge economic disparities between the three countries. Economically Mexico lags way behind, with a Gross National Product only one tenth of that of the USA, while wages in Mexico are only a fraction of those in the United States and Canada (see Table 1). This has given rise to concerns that the NAFTA, by lifting investment restrictions, will simply encourage US industry to move south to take advantage of cheap Mexican labour. This would not only cause job losses in the USA, but also reinforce a low-wage strategy in Mexico.

In the agricultural sector there are huge differences, both in productivity per hectare and in the costs of production. These are particularly worrying in the basic grains industry, upon which most of Mexico's rural population depend for a livelihood (see Table 2). Free trade in these agricultural sectors will enable US and Canadian grain producers to dump their surpluses in Mexico. Mexican peasant producers will be unable to compete, and will be forced to find alternative means of making a living. For many, this will mean leaving the land.

Table 1: *Hourly rates of pay (US$) in the industrial sector (1990)*

Country	Manufacturing	Textile	Electronics
Mexico	1.40	1.27	1.04
USA	10.80	9.74	14.31
Canada	12.30	11.23	13.99

Table 2: *Average yields per hectare and costs of production (CP) between 1985 and 1989*

Country	Maize (tons)	CP (US$)	Beans (tons)	CP (US$)
Mexico	1.7	259	542	641
USA	7.0	93	1.7	220
Canada	6.2	n.a.	1.9	n.a.

(Data from research carried out by Mario B. Monroy for his book *Socios a Sociados en Sociedad: Asimetrias entre Canada, EEUU, Mexico*, Mexico City: RMALC, 1993)

In recognition of the disparities that exist among member countries of the European Union, a Social Development Fund has been established specifically to assist the economic and social development of the weaker economies, such as Portugal, Greece, and Ireland. While this has often been criticised for being inadequate, and has been the cause of considerable controversy, it is a mark of recognition of the social costs of economic union.

Yet, in the NAFTA, where the asymmetries between Mexico and its northern neighbours are so much greater than between any of the countries in the European Union, there has never been any discussion of compensatory financing or social development funding. Indeed, the sums that would have to be involved in order to close the gaps between Mexico and North America would require a level of financing that would be absolutely unacceptable to either the US or Canadian governments.

The democratic deficit

Most people agree that a North American free-trade agreement should be built on democratic principles, yet the way in which the negotiations were conducted has served to reinforce the lack of democracy in Mexico and has undermined democratic decision-making in the USA and Canada.

The ruling Institutional Revolutionary Party (PRI) has been in power in Mexico since 1929.[11] There are numerous, mostly fragmented, opposition parties in Mexico, but until the 1980s the PRI faced little serious opposition, and only in the latter half of that decade did it face opposition capable of defeating it. This came from the National Action Party (PAN) and, to a lesser extent, the Party of the Democratic Revolution (PRD). The PRI's victory in the 1988 elections was widely suspected to have been achieved by fraudulent means.

This political context effectively precluded a democratic debate on NAFTA in Mexico; but even in Canada there was little real consultation. When polled by their government in August 1991, sixty per cent of Canadians declared themselves opposed to the agreement. The Canada-US Free Trade Agreement had provided them with an unsettling education in how corporate-defined trade relations with the USA can affect the social fabric of a nation. However, this verdict on the NAFTA did not deter the Canadian government from pursuing the negotiations. In Mexico President Salinas, by defining the agreement as a treaty, denied the opportunity for a full debate on the issue in the Chamber of Deputies. It was held in the Chamber of Senators, where 61 out of 64 Senators belong to the ruling PRI. He negotiated the agreement following the elections in 1991. The US Administration effectively stifled public debate by pushing the NAFTA through on fast-track legislation, which limited US Congressional consideration of the agreement.[12] The first opportunity for public debate on the actual proposals of the

15

agreement came in 1992, but only after a draft text had been leaked to the public.

Many commentators have compared the process of North American integration with the history of the European Union. It has been pointed out, for example, that as long as Spain, Portugal, and Greece were ruled by dictatorships, they were not welcome to join the community of European nations. Moreover, unlike the European Union, which has incorporated a Social Charter into its plans for further economic integration, discussions on basic human, social, and environmental rights were tacked on to the NAFTA at the last moment, rather than being central to the discussion.

Rural poverty and the NAFTA

Tequisquiapan lies on the edge of a large valley in the State of Queretaro, about three hours north of Mexico City off the main highway to the US border. Attracted by its thermal springs, vineyards, and pleasant climate, tourists have flocked to this small town for years. Most are Mexicans, retreating from the rigours of life in the capital city. But as recession bites, and the Mexican middle classes have had to tighten their belts, the tourist industry has begun to contract. Nowadays business is slack in the town's normally busy restaurants, and many of its hotels are up for sale. Disappearing with them is a major source of employment for the area, reflecting not only the fickle nature of the tourist industry, but also the sorry state of the Mexican economy.

The area surrounding Tequisquiapan is wide, open, arid countryside dotted with cacti and fringed by rocky hills coated with stubby vegetation. The summers are hot and dry and the winter nights bitterly cold. Small, dusty villages are scattered across the valley and the dry, brown, windswept landscape is broken up by green swathes of irrigated grass-land, marking the cattle ranches of the rich. The people of this valley are known for their skills as weavers, but for most it is the land upon which they depend for a livelihood.

Much of this is *ejido* land: communal land farmed by small groups of peasants, whose families benefited from the sweeping land-reform programmes of the 1930s. Corn and beans are the staple crops. On the homesteads there are chickens and sometimes a cow to provide milk for the family.

Rural communities, such as those scattered across this Queretaro valley, still form the backbone of Mexican society. While the government pursued policies of modernisation through import substitution, from the 1940s to 1970s, such communities benefited from a range of subsidies and support policies designed to nurture the country's food-sufficiency programmes. When economic crisis struck and the country was bowled towards structural adjustment and free-market policies, government support for the peasant agricultural sector began to be withdrawn. As of 1995 there will, for the first time in decades, be no guaranteed price for corn. Instead, farmers will receive a payment of 300 Mexican pesos, about US$100, per hectare per year. What they are able to earn in addition to this from their crops will be further threatened by the accelerated pace of liberalisation resulting from the signing of the NAFTA. The gradual dismantling of import restrictions will open Mexico up to cheap US grains and render most Mexican peasant producers uncompetitive. They will have little choice other than to leave the land.

Resisting the drift to the cities

Responding to this crisis is a small regional development and training programme for farmers. The programme, which has several thousand members drawn from the valley communities, is pursuing a strategy of regional self-sufficiency. To this end it promotes a range of activities which include family savings schemes, income-generation projects, technical support for the basic-grains producers, and regional marketing schemes. In this way the organisers hope to help insulate the communities from the external economy which not only threatens their agricultural systems but has also reduced opportunities to earn extra money from the Tequisquiapan tourist industry. They hope that, with the help of the union, people will feel able to stay on the land and not be forced to drift to the cities in search of employment.

The programme organisers do not know if their strategy will be successful in helping rural communities to survive the full onslaught of liberalisation resulting from the NAFTA. The forces against success are powerful. The Mexican government has pledged itself to reducing the rural population from 27 per cent of the economically active population to only 10 per cent by the end of the decade.[13]

Free-market restructuring of the agricultural sector

1985, the year in which the Mexican government had to request further loans from Washington, signalled the start of a complete overhaul of the Mexican agricultural sector. The guidelines for this restructuring were set by the World Bank and the IMF as a condition of further borrowing, and reflected the prevailing free-market orthodoxies of the two institutions. While the restructuring process began in that year, it accelerated in 1988 following the election of Salinas de Gortari as President. He, even more than his predecessor de la Madrid, was committed to the principles of free-market economics and privatisation.

The objectives of the restructuring have evolved over the years in which it has been taking place. The government has promoted a liberalised agricultural sector which is open and responsive to the forces of the free market. Self-sufficiency in food is no longer on the political agenda. From being self-sufficient up until the late 1960s, Mexico now has to import one third of its food needs.[14] Under the free-market model, it is envisaged that the nation's food security will be achieved by its ability to purchase food imports with its agro-industrial export earnings, while the rural peasant population will be absorbed by the growing industrial and service sectors, thus completing Mexico's shift from a Third World agrarian society to a First World industrial nation.

To achieve this 'modernisation' of the agricultural sector, policy reform has concentrated on four main areas:

- the removal of subsidies and price-support mechanisms;
- the privatisation of agricultural parastatal bodies;
- reform of the land-tenure systems;
- and the removal of border restrictions on trade.

With regard to the first area, Mexico's peasant producers used to be able to rely on subsidies to enable them to afford fertilisers, fuel, credit, water, seeds, and crop insurance. However, these are gradually being withdrawn, as are price guarantees for all crops. Government subsidies will henceforward apply to the land itself.

19

The second area concerns the privatisation of agricultural parastatals and the encouragement of agro-industrial investment. In 1990 the government's 'National Programme of Modernisation of the Countryside, 1990-94' was unveiled, announcing the private-sector focus of the new agricultural policies in Mexico. However, even before this announcement, the government had been moving to sell off its various firms and agencies. The restructuring of CONASUPO, the state's food-distribution agency, and Inmecafe, the coffee marketing board, was already under way, and a number of parastatals have since been sold to foreign enterprises, most of which are from the United States. The lifting of investment restrictions through the NAFTA will open the way for further investment by North American corporations.

The third area of policy reform concerns Mexico's land-tenure system. Three fifths of Mexico's agricultural land, approximately 205 million acres, belong to peasant collectives (made up of 2.7 million farmers), known as *ejidos*. The *ejido* lands were distributed to Mexican peasants after the Mexican revolution. The small plots of land could be farmed and passed from generation to generation, but not sold. However, in December 1991 the government approved a constitutional amendment giving the *ejidos* title to communal land with the right to mortgage, lease, or sell it. What this means is that with the sale and consolidation of these plots it will become possible to modernise, industrialise, and increase agricultural production in almost every sector of Mexican agriculture.

The fourth category of policy reforms is directed at the liberalisation of agricultural trade through the removal of border restrictions. Upon joining the multilateral GATT trade accord in 1986, Mexico accelerated its liberalisation policies, opening up its borders to international trade far beyond the terms of the agreement. Highly significant in this was the government's elimination of most import licences (meaning that it no longer had to approve the purchase of foreign commodities). Such policies have paved the way for implementation of the NAFTA. The section which relates to agriculture provides for the immediate removal of all non-tariff barriers to trade (methods such as the imposition of technical or health standards used to limit, or exclude, unwanted goods) through their conversion to tariffs. These will then be eliminated over a period of ten to fifteen years, eventually allowing for the unrestricted movement of agricultural products between the three countries.

Impact on the poor

There is little doubt that the Mexican agricultural sector was in need of reform. Management of the sector had been erratic for many years and had lost its once-clear sense of direction: to support national self-sufficiency in food, through the promotion of small-scale agricultural production. It had suffered from cost-cutting in the austerity years of the early 1980s and had had liberal sums of money poured into it during the boom years of the 1970s. Its priorities had wavered between support for the promotion of food sufficiency through peasant-sector production and support for the promotion of the agro-export industry. There was growing discontent among rural communities over the mismanagement and increasing marginalisation of their sector of the economy.

Erratic management has, undoubtedly, been replaced by clear policy direction, but it is a policy that contributes to the marginalisation and increasing poverty of rural communities. Starved of credit and unable to pay ever-spiralling prices for inputs such as fertilisers, farmers are abandoning new technologies, improved seeds, and chemical inputs, and their productivity is falling. Many farmers are resorting to subsistence agriculture. Others are looking for ways to supplement their income. Frequently this has meant leaving the countryside to seek work in the cities or in the USA. This in itself is contributing to a deepening of rural poverty, as fewer family members, often women and children, are left to carry on the task of subsistence agriculture. Trade liberalisation with North America will add to their difficulties. Its most damaging impact will be on the grains sector. Corn, which is grown on 42 per cent of all arable land in Mexico and by one out of every three farmers, will not be able to compete with the much cheaper US corn. US corn benefits from government support equal to 35 per cent of its production value, compared with a level of support worth only 3 per cent of production value in Mexico. Once these markets are opened, Mexican producers will be at a severe competitive disadvantage.

Overall projections for the number of peasant farmers who will be displaced as a result of these policies vary from 5 to 15 million.[15] Among them will be many of the country's 2.7 million communal farmers. The way has been prepared for them to leave the rural sector, by the reforms to the land-tenure laws which mean they may now own — and thus sell — their land.

In many parts of Mexico, rural communities are struggling to combat spiralling poverty through collective action, in an effort to construct alternative development models. Some are working to promote the concept of regional self-sufficiency. Others are trying to forge 'alternative' trading links with sympathetic consumers in the North, while some are trying organic production in an effort to break into new markets. The despair of Mexico's rural communities, resulting from the failure of their government's policies to address the problems that they face, undoubtedly lies behind the Chiapas rebellion and underlines the need to redirect government policy in favour of the rural poor.

Urban poverty and unemployment

Proponents of the free-market model argue that strengthening the industrial and service sectors of the economy will create employment for those who have lost their jobs or livelihoods as a result of the restructuring of the economy. However, there is overwhelming evidence to suggest that this cannot happen in Mexico, and that the free-market development model is contributing to structural unemployment.

The liberalisation process has bitten hard into the rural sector, but that is not the only place where its effects have been felt. Small and medium-sized businesses in Mexico have also suffered. Once protected by policies designed to nurture import substitution, this sector of the economy, producing goods such as shoes, clothing, textiles, and vehicle parts, thrived and provided important employment opportunities, particularly in urban areas. Faced with increasing levels of competition from imports, many have been forced to close down. The NAFTA, with its strict rules of origin, new rules on trade standards, and its eventual removal of all import restrictions on North American goods, threatens this sector with extinction. With it will go thousands more jobs.

The liberalisation process has attracted investment to Mexico. However, the new style of industrial development, apparent in Mexico City's sprawling industrial suburbs, where highly automated foreign corporations such as Ford and General Motors have set up business, is much less labour-intensive than the type of operation that had previously prevailed. It is argued that the new type of investment will never be able to provide sufficient employment to cater for the vast numbers of people displaced by the restructuring of the economy.

Official government statistics put unemployment levels at 3.5 per cent of the economically active population.[16] Unofficial figures suggest that close to 40 per cent of the population are either unemployed or underemployed. Among these are the hordes of men, women, and children on the streets of Mexico City who are testimony to the extraordinary ingenuity of people in search of ways to survive. Fire-eaters, their faces raw from the heat of the flames, entertain passers-by on the city's highways in the hope of being thrown a few coins. Women and children sit patiently by the roadside, ever-hopeful of selling the few trinkets or crafts laid out before them to passing tourists. Others wash car windscreens, clean shoes, or sell sweets. These are the people who never appear on the government's unemployment register, but equally may never find jobs.

Labour and labour rights

My name is Alma Molina, and I live in Juarez, Mexico with my husband and son. In June 1992, I went to work for Clarostat, a US company, with a plant in Juarez. I was among some 300 workers who made electrical switches and sensors. I earned the Mexican minimum wage, $4.50 for a nine-hour day.

A group of us wanted to improve our working conditions, safety, and wages at Clarostat. We worked with dangerous chemicals, including phenol and epoxy resin, but no masks were provided. The chemicals also irritated our skin. Six of us began to organise a union. We had meetings every two weeks. After a few months, another worker informed on me, and then I was fired. Four other workers were fired one week later. The personnel manager told me I was being fired because I was trying to organise a union. I told them this was unfair, and that I was going to fight this unfair termination. Clarostat then sent me my severance pay.

Shortly after being fired, I was hired by Electrocomponentes, which is a General Electric (GE) Company. The GE logo is on the factory. At that plant, 1,800 workers make wiring for refrigerators sold in the USA. I earned $4.50 for working from 6.30 am to 4.30 pm.

I had been at GE for only seven days when I was called to the personnel office and shown a list with my name on it. This list was kept in a black folder. The personnel man said that he did not know why my name was on the list, but that he would have to fire me anyway. He told me that this was a list of 'undesirable' people, like criminals and drug addicts and thieves. He asked me what kind of criminal I was. I told him that I was not a criminal, but I thought that workers' rights should be respected. I said that maybe this was the reason why I was on the list. He told me to sign a letter of resignation. I would not.

(Extract from the testimony of Alma Molina, *maquiladora* worker, on the subject of violations of workers' rights in Mexico, given before the Subcommittee on Employment, Housing and Aviation House Government Operations Committee, US Congress, 15 July 1993)

Mexico is no stranger to unregulated foreign investment. In 1965 the government instituted the Border Industrialisation Programme, which opened up a 20 km strip along the border with the United States to labour-intensive, export-oriented assembly plants. Since then some 2,000 factories, mainly US-owned, employing half a million Mexican workers, have sprung up, mainly along the border but also in other parts of Mexico. These factories, known as *maquiladoras*, import duty-free materials from the USA. The materials are then processed or assembled, and re-exported back to the United States.

Maquiladoras: exporting profits

The advantage for the companies which own the *maquiladora* plants is that they can maintain productivity levels — but at only a fraction of what it would cost them to do so in the USA. Wages in Mexico are approximately one tenth of those north of the border, and health and safety and environmental regulations, which exist under Mexican law, are hardly ever enforced. As Alma Molina's testimony claims, any attempt by workers to organise to improve conditions is forcefully suppressed; and Mexico's rapidly rising levels of unemployment mean that there is never any shortage of workers to replace the labour activists. As a result, the *maquiladora* zone, a haven for company investment, has some of the poorest living and working conditions in the world and suffers the effects of widespread environmental degradation.

It was to the *maquiladora* zone, as the shape of things to come, that critics of the NAFTA pointed when they challenged the deregulation of trade between Mexico, the United States, and Canada. Workers in the USA fear job losses as companies shift part of their operations south, to take advantage of cheap labour and lax investment regulations. A *Wall Street Journal* poll of 505 senior executives of US manufacturing companies showed that 40 per cent of them would consider shifting some production to Mexico following a free-trade pact.[17] Other studies based on the experience of the European Union predict that between 260,000 and 439,000 jobs could be relocated from the USA to Mexico following a free-trade pact.[18] The agreement could also put a downward pressure on wages in the United States. One economist has predicted that increased competition from Mexican workers will depress the wages of unskilled workers in the USA by an estimated one thousand dollars a year.[19]

Critics of NAFTA in Mexico fear that the agreement will work against democratic reform and will thus lock Mexico into *maquiladora*-style development based on low wages, poor working conditions, and environmental degradation. Key to ensuring that the country remains an attractive investment site for North American companies is the continued repression of independent trade unions. If wages and conditions of employment in Mexico rise as a result of free collective bargaining, the country will lose its competitive advantage.

However, there is little danger of this happening. Labour organising in Mexico is tightly controlled. There is one official union, the CTM (the Confederation of Workers of Mexico). Members of the CTM are obliged to vote for the ruling PRI party, but have no rights to genuine collective bargaining. There is one independent labour union, the Authentic Labour Front (FAT), which is democratically run and unaffiliated to any political party. Not surprisingly, it has a strong following among Mexico's poorly paid workforce and has 40,000 workers organised in 18 Mexican states. As such it is a threat to the *status quo*, but, as Alma Molina's testimony claims and critics of Mexico's human rights allege, they tend to be ruthlessly dealt with:

The victims of human rights violations are most often individuals who have tried to secure union rights or form independent labour unions to improve the abhorrent working conditions in transnational industries. They have been actively targeted: many have been captured, tortured and assassinated.[20]

As a result of such repressive measures, Mexican wages have been kept well below those of South East Asia and in real terms have fallen by 50 per cent over the last ten years.[21]

The labour side-accord

Widespread opposition in the United States to the NAFTA on these grounds led Governor Bill Clinton to commit himself during his Presidential election campaign in October 1992 to the adoption of a parallel side-agreement on labour. This was designed to placate opponents by setting up mechanisms to enforce minimum labour standards. They apply to all three countries, but are particularly directed at the Mexican labour sector. The side-accord was published in August 1993 and came into effect with the main agreement in January 1994.

The accord allows for complaints to be dealt with by the imposition of trade sanctions on matters that relate to the use of child labour, minimum-wage violations, and health and safety regulations. While the side-accord has been welcomed, in that it recognises the need to link international trade regulations with the need to improve workers' conditions, it is widely argued that its main provisions will do little to encourage better working practices in Mexico.

The use of child labour in Mexico is widespread, despite the existence of well-written laws that prohibit it. As many as ten million children work illegally, or subsist as street vendors.[22] However, children are not employed in the *maquila* plants, or other parts of the formal sector of the Mexican economy which will come within the orbit of the NAFTA. The provisions in the side-accord that relate to child labour will, therefore, be impotent in tackling the wider problem.

As for the provision on minimum wages, there is already a legal minimum wage in Mexico. In the formal sector most employers pay slightly above it, thus shifting responsibility for making social-security contributions on to the employee. However, the minimum wage is set so low that it barely constitutes a living wage. At around US$4.50 a day, it is less than the average *hourly* rate in the USA. The health and safety provisions have also been criticised, on the grounds that in Mexico there is no tradition of reporting accidents. Lawyers argue that there would have to be a profound cultural change in Mexico before health and safety legislation could be effective.[23]

However, the side-accord attracted most criticism because it contains no similar provisions on workers' rights. In its preamble the accord recognises the need to promote what it calls 'workers' provisions', such as the freedom of association and the right to collective bargaining. But these are mere obligations to be under-taken by the parties. They are to be backed up not by the threat of trade sanctions, but by fact-finding exercises, and in some cases 'consultations'.

Some unions in the USA now recognise that their best chance of defending US jobs is by encouraging the building of strong, independent labour unions in Mexico, able to defend workers' rights and improve working conditions. This marks a dramatic reversal in their NAFTA strategy, which, when the negotiations were under way, was to oppose the agreement outright on the grounds that it would result in US job losses. At the forefront of this new approach is the United Electrical Workers' Union, which represents about half of all unionised workers in the giant General Electric Corporation. In the last decade GEC has moved 15 of its plants to Mexico, with consequent job losses for workers in the USA.

To help strengthen labour organising in Mexico, the unions are pursuing a twin-track approach. The first (pioneered by the Electrical Workers' Union) is to build a strategic organising alliance with the Mexican Authentic Labour Front, the FAT. The union is subsidising FAT organisers in the border *maquiladoras*, targeting facilities owned by corporations with strong US unions that can put pressure on international headquarters to settle grievances in Mexico. Their second approach is to strengthen those areas of the NAFTA labour side-accord which relate to workers' rights, by filing test cases. The first of these was filed on 14 February 1994 by the United Electrical Workers' Union and the powerful Teamsters' Union. The complaint challenges the firing of over 100 workers in two Chihuahua plants of US-owned companies, General Electric and Honeywell. Most of the fired workers were accused of participating in union activities.[24]

The outcome of the case has yet to be seen. If the ruling is in favour of the union's case and results in the reinstatement of the sacked workers, then the side-accord, for all its weaknesses, could make a significant contribution to an improvement in workers' conditions and pave the way for the strengthening of independent labour organisations in Mexico.

NAFTA and the environment

The environment is a crucial issue for Mexico. Mexico City, home to 18 million people, has the worst atmospheric pollution of any city in the world. Deforestation has reduced Mexico's tropical forests from 27 million to only one million hectares. Eight per cent of land suffers from erosion and 10 per cent from salination. Industry annually generates 115 million tonnes of solid wastes and an undetermined amount of untreated toxic waste, both of which pose a grave threat to public health. Eighty per cent of the rivers are polluted, as well as a large portion of the Gulf of Mexico.[25]

Rampant pollution ...

Some of the worst examples of environmental degradation are along the US-Mexico border. Cheap unorganised labour is not the only attraction of Mexico's *maquiladora* zone for US corporate interests. By moving south, they also escape compliance with US environmental standards. Similar laws exist in Mexico but, as with the country's labour laws, enforcement is weak. By law, Mexican companies are supposed to ship their toxic waste back across the border to the USA. But the heavily polluted local rivers and contaminated water supplies are powerful evidence that many are not doing so. Air pollution is also a serious problem. Cars lack pollution-control devices and travel on unmade-up roads, throwing dust into the air. Added to this is industrial pollution, some of it coming from US furniture makers that moved out of Los Angeles to escape new restrictions on emission standards covering toxic solvents used in paints, stains, and lacquers. Still more comes from local residents who, in the absence of any other way of disposing of it, burn their rubbish.[26]

... and pillaged resources

The US-Mexican border is a concrete example of how unregulated trade can serve to degrade the environment, and it is now widely recognised that complete deregulation poses a grave threat to national and global efforts to protect the environment. Apart from the opportunities it gives companies to flout lax environmental laws, it can also undermine national or local efforts to protect the environment. Free trade would designate any restriction on imports or exports on environmental grounds as a non-tariff barrier to trade, and thus an unacceptable protectionist measure. Likewise free trade would prevent international, national, or local efforts to protect the global commons by, for example, forbidding countries to ban imports of unsustainably produced tropical hardwood in the interests of rain-forest conservation. Such powerful arguments eventually succeeded in forcing the GATT to consider the trade/environment connection within the Uruguay Round, with the result that a trade and environment committee will be established in the new World Trade Organisation. They also brought the issue to prominence in the debate on the NAFTA.

Empty promises

The US Administration labelled the NAFTA as the 'greenest' trade deal so far and, given that previous trade agreements have almost entirely ignored environmental issues, such a claim would not be hard to prove. Its preamble states that the NAFTA partners are committed to 'promote sustainable development ... protect, enhance and enforce worker's rights and to improve working conditions in each country ... and strengthen the development and enforcement of environmental laws'. A major weakness is that the preamble does not go on to define what is meant by 'sustainable development'. However, environmentalists argue that the agreement itself promotes a model of development that posits that wealth must be generated first — wealth which will, in turn, allow future generations to pay for the clean-up. This is in direct contradiction to the view that sustainable development is about meeting the needs of people today without jeopardising the ability of future generations to meet their needs. In short, the NAFTA is a gamble on sustainability.

Four main concerns about the agreement have been voiced by environmentalists.

- The first is that the NAFTA could result in a reduction of environmental regulations to the lowest prevailing standards in the free-trade area. This would come about as a result of the 'harmonisation' of standards which could be used to reduce more restrictive national standards to existing internationally recognised levels.

- The second concern relates to the poor enforcement of environmental laws in Mexico. On the evidence of the *maquiladora* zone, it is easy to see how Mexico could simply become a 'polluter's haven' for those companies which are unwilling to comply with regulations which are enforced in the USA or Canada, but not in Mexico.

- Thirdly there is concern that, given budgetary constraints, there is insufficient funding for Mexican government agencies to deal properly with pollution problems.

- Finally, the NAFTA will inhibit the ability of governments to control exports of natural resources for conservation purposes, with the aim of encouraging domestic processing of raw materials. For Mexico this could mean losing any means of controlling its oil industry.

The environmental side-agreement

As with labour, in response to the criticisms levelled at the agreement on environmental grounds, President Clinton had an environment side-agreement drawn up, in an effort to address the environmental weaknesses in the NAFTA. It provides for the establishment of a tri-national Commission for Environmental Co-operation (CEC) to deal, through a complicated and lengthy process, with disputes between countries regarding lax enforcement of environmental laws. In addition it announced that the USA and Mexico will continue discussion on the financing of infrastructure, such as sewerage systems, in the border region.

However, the side-agreement did little to convince environmentalists. Friends of the Earth have criticised the CEC on the grounds that it lacks teeth. The Commission, it argues, has no power to investigate a complaint, but must rely on evidence supplied by a government. It can draw attention to environmental problems, but cannot offer preventative solutions. Its definition of environmental law is so narrow that it excludes many important areas, including laws regulating the exploitation of natural resources. It places the responsibility for the enforcement of environmental law squarely on the shoulders of governments, thus exempting industry from any obligations.[27]

The side-agreement also resulted in the setting up of a North American Development Bank to help finance environmental and infrastructural projects along the US-Mexican border. The cost of cleaning up the border region has been estimated to be in the region of US$8 billion. The USA and Mexico will both contribute funds to the bank, but Mexico's share of this will be 70 per cent — even though much of the pollution has been caused by US companies flouting Mexico's lax environmental laws.

Free trade — increased protectionism

Critics of the NAFTA argue that it is not, as its name suggests, a free-trade agreement, but a new form of protectionism. While tariff barriers are lowered, the agreement also puts into place new barriers against trade. These, in the way that they are designed, will protect and nurture the interests of large corporations over those of wider society. There are three principal ways in which NAFTA does this: firstly through applying strict rules of origin, secondly through those measures which relate to trade standards, and thirdly through giving increased protection to intellectual property.

Rules of origin

To ensure that the benefits of NAFTA are accorded only to those goods produced in the region, strict rules of origin are laid down in the NAFTA text. These vary by sector. For example, in the car industry 62.5 per cent of parts, labour, and other costs must be added in North America for a car or truck to qualify for lower duties. For computers, only 20 to 40 per cent of a computer's value need be North American to qualify.[28]

This will have a profound impact on the small and medium-sized business sector in Mexico, particularly in the automobile and textile industries. The automobile industry in Mexico is an important source of employment. Companies import components, from countries such as Brazil, take them on to the next stage of assembly, and sell them on to the big, generally US-owned, companies. Under the new rules they will no longer be able to do this, as the assembled car or truck will not meet 'rules of origin' requirements. The same problem faces the textile industry in Mexico, which relies on imports of the raw materials from countries in, for example, Asia.

Technical standards

Chapter 12 of the agreement covers all standards-related measures in relation to trade between the three countries. While encouraging each country to comply with international standards, as set out in the GATT agreement for example, it also permits each party to '... establish and maintain its own standards-related measures relating to environmental, health, safety or other standards-related measures, including measures to prohibit the importation of products failing to meet those standards or technical regulation'.

Some, particularly environmentalists, welcome this provision in the NAFTA, because it ensures that each country has the right to adopt more stringent, science-based standards to achieve a chosen level of protection. However, it has been criticised on the grounds that it could, just as easily, lead to unjust protectionist measures which work in favour of the larger, more powerful corporations and against the interests of the smaller, more vulnerable, companies.

In the USA, the setting of technical standards is done by private companies. Furthermore, each state has autonomy over its standards-setting, so standards may vary between states. If one particular company wants to keep a certain competing product out of the state, it simply ensures that the technical standards (relating to the environment, health, safety, etc.) are set higher than the product in question can match.

Particularly vulnerable to these measures are small Mexican businesses. For example, one Mexican co-operative was enjoying a niche market in the USA for its fruit-juice exports. The technical standards were suddenly raised and the co-operative lost its market. Such measures will undoubtedly contribute to the difficulties faced by the small-business sector in Mexico.

Intellectual property rights

For many, the most controversial chapter of the NAFTA, and the one that most blatantly favours corporate interests over those of wider society, is that which relates to Intellectual Property Rights. Since the 1980s, under pressure from US industry, the US administration has been pushing to have intellectual property rights (IPRs) included in trade agreements. As a result, a detailed code on intellectual property, known as the TRIPS — Trade Related Intellectual Property Rights — Agreement, has been included in the new GATT agreement, and a very similar code appears in the NAFTA. Thus Intellectual Property Rights have been placed firmly on the international trade agenda.

Intellectual Property Rights concern the rules governing patents, trademarks, and copyrights, which are normally held by private corporations. Intellectual property has become an issue of critical importance to US corporations. While some sectors of the US economy, such as manufacturing, are in decline, the USA still maintains its dominance in information and technology-intensive industries. The inclusion of IPRs in trade agreements is specifically designed to ensure that they will be able to maintain this dominance.

The fundamental problem with the inclusion of IPRs in trade agreements is that they protect the 'rights' of corporate owners without recognising corresponding obligations to society as a whole. In particular it restricts the transfer of technology to less developed countries wishing to adapt technology to their own development needs. The IPR chapter of the NAFTA will, therefore, have a negative effect on Mexico's development prospects.

Basically the NAFTA provisions on IPRs strengthen the ability of corporations to maintain exclusive ownership of a design, product, or process. The most immediate effects of this will be felt in the pharmaceutical industry. Mexico, like many other countries , has developed a generic drugs industry which reproduces the tried and tested brands of the major drugs companies and sells them on the local market for a fraction of the cost. Under NAFTA it will no longer be possible for them to do this. Products developed by the major drugs companies will be protected from copying by tight patenting provisions, and as a result the Mexican people will no longer have access to affordable drugs.

The IPR provisions will, of course, extend beyond the drugs industry. The NAFTA also opens the ways for extending patenting laws to life forms: plants, animals, genetic materials, and even life forms derived from the human body. For agriculture:

Life form patents will result in farmers being denied their traditional rights to save seed (because) planting seeds without paying royalties is making an unauthorised copy of a patented product. Farmers will be forced to pay royalties for every seed and farm animal derived from patented stock, forced to become more dependent on fertilisers, pesticides and the machinery made by the same companies who collected the traditional seeds in the first place and now sell back the chemically-dependent derivatives.[29]

The NAFTA's provisions on intellectual property are novel and important not only for their broad scope, but for their enforcement procedures. Unlike other sections of the NAFTA, including those on labour and the environment, clear procedures are laid down for the enforcement of intellectual property rights, including border measures which prevent the entry of goods alleged to infringe IPRs.[30]

The protection of transnationals' patents, provided for by both the NAFTA and the GATT, will enhance the power of high-technology firms based in industrialised countries. The costs of this for the poorer countries could be high. It has been estimated that if Northern transnational corporations were to collect all the royalties they claim are owed to them by developing countries, the drain of wealth from the South to the North would be upwards of US$100 billion a year.[31] As one critic of IPR provisions pointed out, rules on intellectual property rights 'benefit only the powerful ... Although (they would) apply equally to all nations, one can argue that equal treatment among unequals is profoundly inequitable.'[32]

Impact on the economy

The restructuring of the Mexican economy that preceded Mexico's accession to the NAFTA has not prompted the economic recovery promised by its government. In 1993 economic growth, at 0.4 per cent, was outstripped by population growth for the first time since 1988.[33] Mexico still had a substantial trade deficit, of US$13.6 billion (£9.3 billion) in 1993, and an external debt in excess of US$124 billion.[34]

A World Bank report published in February 1994 praised Mexico for having followed the Bank's advice on economic policy, but expressed concern over its slow economic growth and low savings rate. It concludes that the high current-account deficit and modest improvements in productivity 'raise concern about the sustainability of economic growth'. The Bank attributes the low economic growth to the 'substitution of foreign goods for domestically produced goods'. Implicit in this is an acknowledgment of the importance of the small-business sector in Mexico and the devastating impact that the restructuring has had on it.

The Bank recommends further reforms in four areas: the legal system, to make it easier for private-sector development; the labour sector, to increase the quality of the labour force and establish a more flexible labour market; environmental policy, for which it recommends mandatory fines for lack of enforcement in compliance with environmental law; and ways in which the provision of infrastructure could be improved.[35]

It appears that Mexico's free-market restructuring is not only failing the poor, but is also failing to produce economic growth.

NAFTA and global economic integration

There are two ways to view the NAFTA. One is that it is of little significance, given the degree of integration that had already taken place between the USA and Mexico under the free-market reforms instigated by the de la Madrid and Salinas administrations in the twelve years before the agreement came into effect. Viewed from this perspective, the NAFTA is simply a way of formalising and speeding up that process of integration. On the other hand, the NAFTA can be seen as very significant, as it will lock into place the liberalisation measures already taken by the Mexican government, making it difficult for future governments to change the free-market orientation of Mexico's economic policies. It will mean that Mexican foreign policy will be formulated in the shadow of the NAFTA, and it will shift power away from the government and into the hands of the corporate sector. Most significantly, it signals the start of a new era of global political and economic relations that will have a profound impact on countries throughout the developing world.

Global economic liberalisation is at the heart of the US administration's economic policy objectives. It has been pursuing this objective in two ways. The first is through the GATT. But, as the seven years that it took to complete the Uruguay Round negotiations prove, multilateral trade arrangements can be slow and problematic; so the USA is also pursuing a second route: economic liberalisation through a series of bilateral deals. The first of these was with Canada, and the second with Mexico through the NAFTA, the provisions of which are similar in many ways to those contained in the Uruguay Round agreement.

For the US administration, the NAFTA is simply the first stage of its wider policy objective of creating a hemispheric free-trade zone 'stretching from the port of Anchorage to the Tierra del

Fuego'. The Enterprise of the Americas Initiative (EAI), announced by US President George Bush in June 1990, is a three-pronged programme, designed first to create a hemispheric free-trade zone, second to promote private investment in the region, and third to facilitate renegotiation of official debts owed to the US government, including provisions for 'debt-for-nature' swaps.[36]

From the outset President Bush made it clear that his offer of expanded trade, investment, and debt renegotiation through the EAI would be open only to those countries that demonstrate a commitment to free-market economic reform by undertaking structural adjustments such as liberalising their foreign-investment laws, privatising state-owned companies, and deregulating foreign trade. Mexico's whole-hearted embrace of such policies made it a natural first candidate for this scheme.

Demonstrating that such policies have cross-party support in the USA, President Clinton told a meeting in New York, shortly before the NAFTA was signed: 'We see this not as an exclusive agreement, but as part of the building blocks of a framework of continually expanding global trade.' He went on to say that the 'NAFTA could lead the way to a new partnership with Chile, with Argentina, with Colombia, with Venezuela, with a whole range of countries in Latin America (that) have embraced democracy and market economics.'[37]

There is no shortage of countries in Latin America and the Caribbean wishing to demonstrate their commitment to free-market economic reform and join the EAI. Since the beginning of the 1990s, barriers against foreign trade and investment have been torn down in country after country, leading to a boom in intra-regional trade. Currently there are five large trade pacts in the region (see Table 3), in addition to several smaller, bi-national or tri-national free-trade pacts. By January 1992 the United States had signed 30 Framework Agreements with Latin American govern-ments. Only Cuba, Haiti, and Suriname have not been included. Chile, the pioneer in market reform in Latin America, is next in line to join the NAFTA, with negotiations already under way.

Table 3: *Integration and trade in the Americas*[38]

Name of pact	Population (millions)	GDP (US$ bn)	Intra-regional trade (US$ bn)
NAFTA (1994)	**363**	**6,838.7**	**267.0**
USA	(250)	5,950.7	
Canada	(27)	569.0	
Mexico	(86)	319.0	
Mercosur (1991)	**197**	**679.9**	**7.0**
Argentina		228.8	
Brazil		434.0	
Paraguay		5.7	
Uruguay		11.4	
G-Three (1994)	**148**	**432.1**	**1.4**
Mexico		319.0	
Colombia		52.0	
Venezuela		61.1	
Andean Pact (1969)	**97**	**177.1**	**1.9**
Bolivia		6.1	
Ecuador		12.7	
Peru		45.2	
Venezuela		61.1	
Colombia		52.0	
Central America Common Market (1960)			
	27.8	**27.7**	**n.d.**
Costa Rica		6.5	
El Salvador		6.0	
Guatemala		10.5	
Honduras		3.1	
Nicaragua		1.6	
CARICOM (1973)	**5.4**	**12.6**	**n.a.**

(Antigua, Bahamas, Barbados, Belize, Dominica, Grenada, Guyana, Jamaica, Montserrat, St Kitts-Nevis, St Lucia, St Vincent-Grenadines, Trinidad and Tobago)

These framework agreements are not legally binding, but they do signal an intention to pursue further negotiations. Their preambles list principles such as mutual friendship, co-operation within GATT, intent to lower tariff and non-tariff barriers against trade, recognition of the role of private investment, the importance of providing adequate protection for intellectual property rights, and respect for labour rights. Six similar agreements have been signed with members of the Association of South East Asian Nations (ASEAN): Brunei, Malaysia, Indonesia, the Philippines, Singapore, and Thailand. At ASEAN meetings held in July 1992, both US and Canadian officials 'floated the idea of future linkages' with NAFTA, thus demonstrating its global significance.[39]

Towards sustainable economic development

Governments throughout Latin America are queuing up to join the NAFTA. Many are able to display impressive credentials, demonstrating their commitment to free-market economics. Yet Mexico's experience clearly shows the potential flaws in this model of development. Its government's adoption of related policies, crowned by its accession to the NAFTA, has resulted in increased poverty and environmental degradation and, so far at least, has failed to produce significant economic growth. Such results justify a critical re-examination of the model and a search for alternative development models.

In the negotiations that led to the adoption of the NAFTA, the broad-based Mexican, Canadian, and US coalitions which oppose it considered alternative policies that could promote sustainable development and respect basic rights. Their policy recommendations included the following key elements:[40]

1 In recognition of people's need for basic self-reliance in food stocks, agricultural policies should be directed to:

- limiting international trade in food to products that complement domestic production;

- eliminating subsidies that systematically encourage over-production and export dumping, and implementing subsidies designed to encourage food self-reliance and ecologically sound agricultural practices.

2 To ensure that basic workers' rights are respected, legislation should:

- guarantee the rights of all workers to be represented by independent trade unions; to participate in collective bargaining; to go on strike;

- prohibit the use of forced or child labour;
- guarantee basic benefits such as job security, unemployment insurance, workers' compensation, pensions, and a safe working environment.

3 To help to safeguard the environment:

- agricultural producers should be guaranteed returns high enough to sustain small-scale, diversified farms to encourage sustainable agricultural production;
- funds should be set aside to rehabilitate areas adversely affected by commercial activities;
- international trade agreements should contain clauses that allow any party to take action necessary to protect the environment, for example by establishing export or import restrictions and the use of subsidies, to prevent or remedy adverse environmental effects and/or conserve natural resources.

4 Investment policies should respect the rights of governments to choose their own development priorities, and allow them to:

- favour locally-owned, community-oriented investments over foreign investors when licensing operations or allocating finances;
- screen all foreign investments and takeovers to ensure their compatibility with the host country's economic and social goals.

5 Finance for local development initiatives and poverty-alleviation measures should be made available by:

- reducing the debt burden of developing countries.

6 Laws governing Intellectual Property Rights should recognise the rights of the broader society by:

- recognising the sovereign right of countries to establish their own patent and copyright systems and to adapt technology to uses appropriate to their stage of development;

- prohibiting the patenting of life forms such as plant and animal species and biological materials.

7 With the NAFTA in place, priority should be given to:

- supporting networking activities between social organisations and non-government organisations in Mexico and those in other countries waiting to join the NAFTA, to help them press for policies that will promote sustainable economic development and protect basic rights along the lines suggested above;

- increasing poverty-focused aid to Mexico by raising public awareness of the situation of the poor in Mexico;

- supporting efforts to strengthen the provisions contained in the Labour and Environmental Side-agreements.

Notes

1 From an article by Charles Lawrence in New York, sent to *The Daily Telegraph*, dated 3 January 1994.

2 Economist Intelligence Unit: *Mexico Country Profile* 1991-92.

3 Tom Barry: *Mexico: A Country Guide*, The Inter-Hemispheric Education Resource Center, Albuquerque, New Mexico, 1992, p.292.

4 ibid, p.81.

5 IDOC Internazionale: 'The Dream of NAFTA-nuggets', July-September 1993/3.

6 Barry 1992, op. cit., p.119.

7 Cavanagh, Gershman, Baker, Helmke: *Trading Freedom — How Free Trade Affects our Lives, Work and Environment*, Institute for Food and Development Policy, California, USA, 1992, p.38.

8 NGO Working Group on the World Bank: 'Structural Adjustment in Mexico: A Grass Roots Perspective', draft report, April 1993, p.26.

9 *Resource Centre Bulletin* No 23, Albuquerque, New Mexico.

10 World Bank 1989, cited in Barry 1992, op. cit., p.96.

11 At that time it was known as the National Revolutionary Party (PNR). In 1938 it was renamed the Party of the Mexican Revolution (PRM) and in 1946 it was renamed once again as the Institutional Revolutionary Party (PRI).

12 The Development Group for Alternative Policies: *Look Before You Leap: What You Should Know About a North American Free Trade Agreement*, Washington DC: Development GAP, 1991.

13 Interview with Luis Hernandez on 19 January 1994, quoting newspaper reports dating back to January 1993.

14 *Resource Centre Bulletin* No 23, Spring 1991, Albuquerque, New Mexico.

15 Ecumenical Coalition for Economic Justice, Ontario: *Ecumenical Justice Report*, Vol. 2, No. 3, 'Ethical Reflections on North American Integration', October 1991.

16 Statistic given by Mantel Garcia Urrutia in interview on 21 January 1994.

17 *Resource Centre Bulletin* No 31/32, Albuquerque, New Mexico.

18 The Development Gap for Alternative Policies, 1991, op. cit.

19 *Resource Centre Bulletin* No 31/32.

20 Common Frontiers: Project on Human Rights and Economic Integration, August 1992.

21 Opening Statement by Chairman Colin Peterson at the hearing of the Subcommittee on Employment, Housing and Aviation at the US Congress, 15 July 1993.

22 Ecumenical Coalition for Economic Justice, October 1991, op. cit.

23 Interview with Mexican labour lawyer, Arturo Alcalde, 19 January 1994.

24 John Ross: 'On the offensive — now that NAFTA's a fact, US labour unions strike back', *El Financiero International*, 14 March 1994.

25 Ecumenical Coalition for Economic Justice, October 1991, op. cit.

26 B. Coote: *The Trade Trap: Poverty and the Global Commodity Markets*, Oxford: Oxfam (UK and Ireland), 1992, p.134.

27 Friends of the Earth, Washington office, press release: 'Environmental Side Agreement Falls Short of Fixing NAFTA's Flaws', September 1993.

28 IMF: *Mexico: The Strategy to Achieve Sustained Economic Growth*, Occasional Paper 99, IMF, Washington DC, September 1992, p.32.

29 Beth Burrows, Washington Biotechnology Action Council, quoted in *Which Way for the Americas: Analysis of NAFTA Proposals and the Impact on Canada*, published by the Canadian Centre for Policy Alternatives, November 1992, p.40.

30 Ian Robinson: *North American Trade as if Democracy Mattered*, Canadian Centre for Policy Alternatives, Ottawa, 1993.

31 'Canada and the Enterprise for the Americas Initiative', draft paper by The Development GAP, Washington DC.

32 GATT-Fly: *Free Trade, Self Reliance and Economic Justice*, Ecumenical Commission for Economic Justice, Ontario, 1987.

33 *Financial Times*, 22 February 1994.

34 The Economist Intelligence Unit, *Mexico Country Report*, First Quarter 1994.

35 *Financial Times*, 22 February 1994.

36 Ecumenical Coalition for Economic Justice, Ontario: *ECEJ Background Paper* No. 1, 'Overview for the Enterprise of the Americas Initiative', May 1993.

37 *US/Latin Trade — The Magazine of Commerce in the Americas*, January 1994.

38 ibid.

39 Ecumenical Coalition for Economic Justice, May 1993, op. cit.

40 Outlined in the statement '51 Alternatives to NAFTA', published in *Economic Justice Report*, Volume 4, No. 1, April 1993, by the Ecumenical Coalition for Economic Justice, Ontario.

Further reading from Oxfam

The Trade Trap: Poverty and the Global Commodity Markets
Belinda Coote
1992, 224 pages, paperback: ISBN 0 85598 135 0,
hardback: ISBN 0 85598 134 2

The Trade Trap shows how the terms of trade between North and South put poor farmers at an impossible disadvantage. It explains the problems created by trade blocs, the workings of the futures markets, the role played by multinational corporations, and the failure of UNCTAD and the General Agreement on Tariffs and Trade to protect the interests of developing nations. Illustrated with case studies from many of the 70 countries where Oxfam supports communities of poor producers, including Mexico.

'A tour de force! Everything you need to know about trade, with a wealth of case studies.' — Michael Barratt Brown, Chair of Third World Information Network (TWIN) and Twin Trading.

A Buyer's Market: Global Trade, Southern Poverty, and Northern Action
David Dalton
1992, up-dated 1994, 16 pages, paperback ISBN 0 85598 280 2

A short and simple guide to the complexities of world trade, which explains why countries that depend on the export of raw commodities can't win under the present system.

Other books in the series

The **Insight** series offers concise and accessible analysis of issues that are of current concern to the international community.

Paying for Health
Poverty and Structural Adjustment in Zimbabwe
Jean Lennock
ISBN 0 85598 293 4, 40 pages, August 1994

Jean Lennock shows how the most vulnerable sections of society carry the burden of structural adjustment when a government adopts the World Bank's advice to introduce user–fees for health care.

Rwanda
An Agenda for International Action
Guy Vassall–Adams
ISBN 0 85598 299 3, 72 pages, October 1994

Guy Vassall–Adams investigates the background to the genocide and refugee crisis which devastated Rwanda in 1994, and explores the reasons why the international community intervened too late to prevent the tragedy. The book argues for radical reform and proper funding of the UN's peacekeeping and emergency capacities, and presents specific recommendations for action.

Oxfam (UK and Ireland) publishes a wide range of books, manuals, and resource materials for specialist, academic, ad general readers. For a free catalogue, please write to Oxfam Publishing, Oxfam House, 274 Banbury Road, Oxford OX2 7DZ, UK.

Insight books are produced by Oxfam UK and Ireland as part of its advocacy programme on behalf of poor communities. They are co-published with other members of the International Oxfam group. For more information, contact your National Oxfam:

Oxfam America
25 West Street
Boston MA 0211 1206
USA
Tel: 1 617 482 1211
Fax: 1 617 728 2594

Oxfam Canada
Suite 300
294 Albert Street
Ottawa, Ontario K1P 6E6
Canada
Tel: 1 613 237 5236
Fax: 1 613 237 0524

Community Aid Abroad
156 George Street
Fitzroy
Victoria
Australia
Tel: 61 3 289 9444
Fax: 61 3 419 5318

Oxfam New Zealand
Room 101, La Gonda House
203 Karangahape Road
Auckland, New Zealand
Tel: 64 9 358 1480
Fax: 64 9 358 1481

Oxfam Hong Kong
Ground Floor 3B
June Garden
28 Tung Chau Street
Tai Kok Tsui
Kowloon, Hong Kong
Tel: 852 3 916305
Fax: 852 789 9545

The International Oxfams are a group of autonomous, non-profit development agencies. They work to overcome poverty and social injustice through the empowerment of partner organisations and communities to achieve sustainable development or livelihoods, and to strengthen civil society in any part of the world, irrespective of nationality, race, political system, religion, or colour. They are Oxfam America, Oxfam Belgium, Oxfam Canada, Community Aid Abroad (in Australia), Oxfam Hong Kong, NOVIB (in the Netherlands), Oxfam Quebec, and Oxfam United Kingdom and Ireland. The name Oxfam comes from the OXford Committee for FAMine relief, founded in Oxford, England in 1942.

    Insight books are available through Oxfam UK and Ireland's book distributors.

.